heal your life with Reiki

Sandi Leir-Shuffrey

T0352137

Hodder Education

Hodder Education is an Hachette UK company

First published in UK 2011 by Hodder Education.

This edition published 2011.

Copyright © 2011 Sandi Leir-Shuffrey

The moral rights of the author have been asserted.

Database right Hodder Education (makers).

British Library Cataloguing in Publication Data: a catalogue record for
this title is available from the British Library.

10 9 8 7 6 5 4 3 2 1

The publisher has used its best endeavours to ensure that any website
addresses referred to in this book are correct and active at the time of going
to press. However, the publisher and the author have no responsibility for the
websites and can make no guarantee that a site will remain live or that the
content will remain relevant, decent or appropriate.

The publisher has made every effort to mark as such all words which it
believes to be trademarks. The publisher should also like to make it clear that
the presence of a word in the book, whether marked or unmarked, in no way
affects its legal status as a trademark.

Every reasonable effort has been made by the publisher to trace the copyright
holders of material in this book. Any errors or omissions should be notified in
writing to the publisher, who will endeavour to rectify the situation for any
reprints and future editions.

Hachette UK's policy is to use papers that are natural, renewable
and recyclable products and made from wood grown in sustainable
forests. The logging and manufacturing processes are expected to
conform to the environmental regulations of the country of origin.

www.hoddereducation.co.uk

Typeset by MPS Limited, a Macmillan Company.
Printed in Great Britain

I dedicate this book to my sister Jane, whose courage and determination in the face of adversity are inspirational, and to Max Kay – a miracle Reiki baby.

Contents

1

what is Reiki?

We have all experienced stress in our lives. In order to be happy and healthy we need to have a quiet mind, calm emotions and a relaxed body. We need time in solitude in which to reflect and restore vitality.

'Reiki' is the Japanese word for 'universal life force'. It is the energy within and around us. The 'Usui Shiki Ryoho', the original Western form of Reiki, is a simple, practical technique for hands-on healing that can be easily learnt by anyone and used in everyday life.

After a short course it is possible to apply Reiki in a full body treatment to family members, friends, pets and even as a personal self-treatment. Further instruction can activate deeper mental and emotional healing that brings about spiritual change and self-mastery. Anyone can learn this simple technique for the purpose of healing on all levels.

It is very hard to describe Reiki. It is as hard as describing the taste of a strawberry to someone who has never eaten one. Once the strawberry is in the mouth then there needs to be no explanation. Reiki answers all its own questions once the experience is felt.

Reiki is not ...

* an organization
* a religion
* a cult
* a dogma
* a mystery
* intellectual
* learnt with the mind
* difficult to learn
* something you forget easily
* harmful in any way
* complicated
* exclusive
* invasive
* a commodity
* channelling
* to do with spirits and entities
* limited in use
* cranky
* New Age
* inaccessible
* costly
* a cure all
* a moral

Reiki is ...

* Rei – Universal, Ki – Life Force
* transmitted through initiation by a fully qualified, registered Master

* light in motion/energy in motion
* love of the creator
* abundant and naturally available at many levels to suit the individual needs
* intelligent and creative
* the source of all things
* a powerful healing process
* empowering and self-empowering
* unlimited
* effective in chronic and acute illness
* a catalyst for change
* the harnessing of external energy to enhance the quality of internal energy
* constant
* dynamic
* transformative
* easily learnt
* easily applied for self-treatment and to family, friends and pets
* effective for all illnesses and side-effects of medication
* a balancing force of spirit, mind, emotion and body
* holistic
* the greatest pain reliever and healer of wounds
* a healer of the soul
* permanent
* a spiritual journey
* the application of spiritual power to bring about happiness
* meditative
* energizing
* restorative
* calmative
* expansive
* energy in perfect balance
* a profound experience
* a healer of hearts
* a true friend
* a gift

Reiki is an accessible hands-on healing technique that enables you to help yourself. It is a giving and receiving process. It opens the mind to an inherent knowledge and understanding of how the body is created, what sustains it and what destroys it prematurely. Its most immediate aspect is that of pain relief and healing illness. It is not until we have a physical problem that begins to restrict the way we live and what we want to do that we begin a search for a way of balance. For many people the initial search is at the doctor's surgery. Often we feel it is enough to take some medicine for the symptom and wait for the problem to be cured. But many times this does not happen. We seem to get worse or, at least, find no respite from the condition of pain. At some point we may realize that treating the symptoms with drugs is not the answer we want, especially when some of these drugs actually make us feel worse. We end up in a cycle of dependency on the doctor, the medication and even on the illness itself; it is who we have become. There comes a time when we feel, deep down, that there is an answer, a simple remedy for our condition. It is not until we begin to look within and see that we may be creating this condition in some way, or at least can affect it in some way ourselves, that we wake up to the possibility of healing rather than curing.

By treating someone else we are, in effect, assisting in the reclamation of their personal power. Reiki practice is like an offering, an extension of the vital energetic spirit, that is drawn through the hands. Healing occurs as an interaction between the energy body of the receiver and the unlimited external Life Force drawn in via the practitioner. The energy body, also referred to as the subtle body or the energy field, is the electromagnetic vitality of each individual person that extends for beyond the physical body. The energy field reacts instantly to any changes in feeling, thought or chemistry, expanding through relaxation that which has contracted through stress and tension.

Reiki heals the wounds both seen and unseen. It is therefore mystical in origin yet not a mystery. It is a simple power that we, as a race, have forgotten because of the incessant internal dialogue and our compulsive need for doing. Reiki is the Awakener.

A light shed on simplicity. A way through the pain into profound understanding of purpose.

Reiki lessens swelling, bruising, bleeding and blistering. It repairs damaged tissue, scar tissue, tension and trauma in the cells due to surgery, replenishes the flow of communication between the nerve cells, and purifies the body by increasing the elimination of toxins.

Healing can be subtle and slow or it can be tremendous and instant. Whatever our expectation of it, it is pretty much guaranteed not to be like that. No matter what form the healing takes, we are always pleasantly surprised at how close to us the remedy was all along. Sometimes the medicine is needed, sometimes operations are needed, sometimes our illness will not disappear as we would hope, but healing can still take place to give back a quality of life that is empowering rather than dependent.

2

the history of Reiki

The background and origins of Reiki are important in understanding the traditions of this unique method of healing. The lineage, or pathway of teachers, down which the technique is passed determines the purity and simplicity to create effective learning for the student. The stillness and silence already rests within each one of us. Practice is the key to regaining that equilibrium within ourselves. We need to question the technique, gain some knowledge and feel its effects in our daily lives before the understanding is complete.

Reading the journey of people who are now teachers we see that Reiki comes to us when we are in need; some will walk on by and some will embrace it.

The true story of Reiki is actually unclear, as the one passed down to me has since been proved to be quite fabricated. I shall begin with the story that was given by Hawayo Takata, who brought Reiki to the West, and follow with the latest research, possibly also somewhat fictional. Myth and legend abound in Eastern history.

It is believed that Hawayo Takata, whose identity is revealed in this story, adapted the truth to make Reiki more appealing to the West as a Christian society. This is how she told it.

Dr Usui

At the end of the nineteenth century there lived a man called Dr Mikao Usui. He lived in a monastery in Kyoto, Japan. It is said that he was a Christian professor of Theology at Doshisha University. At the time of the graduation of his students, Dr Usui was asked the question, 'How, exactly, did Jesus heal?' He could not give a clear answer as he too had lived on belief and trust in the Bible stories as being true. He resigned from his post at the college and went in search of an answer.

He studied many other scriptures apart from Christian ones. He travelled to America and spent seven years in Chicago where he received a Doctorate degree in Scripture at its university. He eventually returned to Japan where he learnt the ancient language of Sanskrit, with its origins in India, and began reading the Scriptures that describe Japanese Buddhism. He spent much time with monks in a Buddhist monastery reading these ancient texts and learning the sutras and mantras. One day he happened upon something that greatly excited him. There, in the Scriptures, was a passage on healing containing a formula written in symbolic form. The monks explained that their focus was on the spiritual aspect of healing through Buddhism: as the healing of the mind and body were not their primary focus, the symbols were no longer understood by them.

Dr Usui knew the symbols were what he was looking for. They were the keys to the healing ways of the Buddha, Jesus and all others, yet there were no instructions. He recognized them as being very sacred and special. In order to understand them better he decided to use his experience of deep meditation to learn the essence from within himself as triggered by each symbol.

Symbols are very powerful tools. They are keys to unlock and give us access to other levels of consciousness. They contain within their simple structure the whole content of their form and the process which they activate. Dr Usui understood the symbols but not their form, so he took them with him into deep meditation on a nearby holy mountain, Mount Kurama. He sat by a stream with no food and placed before him 21 stones to count the days. He told the monks that in 21 days he would either have found the answer or, if not, they could collect his dead body.

The twenty-first day came and Dr Usui threw away the last stone. At first he felt he had not achieved his goal, but as he surrendered and accepted whatever outcome was to be, he saw a great ball of light rushing towards him. It seemed to knock him into another state of consciousness. In his mind's eye, as if on a screen, he saw each symbol in a golden bubble of light. He held on to each image until an understanding washed through him. When all the symbols had passed through in this way, they had burned themselves into his memory.

Dr Usui arose feeling changed in some way. He came down the mountain feeling surprisingly well and strong. However, he tripped on a rock, stubbing his toe. His immediate reaction was to put his hands there. He noticed how quickly the pain subsided and the bleeding stopped. He had begun the task of gathering evidence that something had taken place.

As he descended the mountain he stopped at a stall selling breakfast. The vendor, realizing that Dr Usui had been fasting, told him to rest and wait for the preparation of a special light meal for his delicate and empty stomach. Dr Usui rested under a tree. The meal was brought out by the young daughter of the vendor who was obviously in much pain due to a swollen tooth abcess. He asked if he could place his hands gently on her face and as he did so the pain subsided and the swelling disappeared. Dr Usui realized that something truly special had happened to him.

He spent the next seven years living among the beggars in the beggars' quarters of Kyoto but realized that they quickly returned to their old ways. When he asked them why they had not moved on with their new-found health they replied, 'This is who we are, what we were born to be. It is all we know.' Dr Usui was sad but realized that healing the physical is not enough. A mental, spiritual attitude is needed also. So he began to teach the Five Precepts of Reiki.

Hawayo Takata translates the Precepts as:

* Just for today do not anger.
* Just for today do not worry.
* Earn your living honestly.
* Honour your parents, elders and teachers.
* Give gratitude to every living thing and every situation.

The modern-day version of the story is that Dr Usui was a Buddhist monk living in a Buddhist monastery with access to the sutras and scriptures in Sanskrit. It is also said that he never attended Chicago University. Some people say he travelled in India and met Tibetan Masters.

It is more likely that he was a Buddhist monk and that Takata adapted the story to be accepted in America. The beauty of oral tradition is that it evolves but it evolves only at the level of consciousness of the story teller. Whatever the story – only Usui knows the truth – I have seen Reiki work. It is a definite power that works through the hands, and the transmissions activate this power without a doubt when performed correctly.

Dr Hayashi

Dr Usui saw the need to look for people who would honour the teaching as precious and have the desire for change. He met a remarkable man called Dr Chujiro Hayashi who was not only a retired Naval Officer but also an aristocrat. Dr Hayashi was keen to assist in healing, having witnessed the destruction of war first hand. He was initiated into Reiki and set up a clinic in Tokyo called Shina No Machi.

When Dr Usui's life was drawing to an end he recognized Hayashi as the Master of Reiki and charged him with keeping the essence of his teachings pure, intact and in their original form. Hayashi agreed to this and made extensive records to demonstrate that Reiki finds the source of physical symptoms, fills the being with vitality and restores the person into wholeness.

Hawayo Takata

In 1935 a lady called Hawayo Takata came to Dr Hayashi's clinic having been diagnosed with many ills, including a tumour for which she was about to undergo an operation. Takata had lived in Hawaii until, in her mid-twenties, her husband died suddenly leaving her grief stricken and alone with two small children. The grief created such illness in her that a tumour formed. However, when she returned to Japan for an operation a voice inside her said, 'There is another way'. She was directed to Dr Hayashi's clinic where she was treated every day for eight months, by which time she had fully recovered. She became a dedicated student, working in the clinic but not learning Reiki as, being a woman, she was not allowed. Over the years she showed a deep commitment to Reiki and eventually Hayashi broke with tradition and initiated her into First Degree.

During the Second World War Hayashi was called up to fight the Americans. Being a Reserve Naval Officer his first duty was to his country and therefore to fight. Being a Universal Healer his duty was also to heal all beings and see them as one. His dilemma was so great that he gathered together all his family and colleagues for a meeting. At the meeting he declared Takata would carry on the lineage and teach Reiki as a Master, keeping the original form and essence pure and simple. He then said, 'There is no such thing as death, only great change' and left his body. His body fell back. He had gone into transition. The mark of enlightenment and lack of stress showed in the fact that his body did not decay as a normal body would. It remained unchanged for many weeks. (This also happened to the great sage Paramahansa Yogananda.)

Takata took Reiki back to Hawaii and introduced her gift to the Western world. She died in 1980 having trained 22 Reiki Masters.

The 22 Masters made by Takata were:

* Wanja Twan
* Barbara Ray
* Mary McFadden
* Fran Brown
* Iris Ishikuro
* Virginia Samdahl
* Shimobu Saito (Takata's sister)
* Phyllis Lei Furumoto (Takata's grand-daughter)
* Paul Mitchell
* Seiji Takimori
* Bethel Phaigh
* Barbara McCullogh
* George Arak
* Dorothy Baba
* Ursula Baylow
* Rick Bockner
* Barbara Brown
* Patricia Ewing
* Beth Gray
* John Gray
* Harry Kubai
* Ethel Lombardi

Wanja Twan

Wanja Twan is Swedish and lives in British Columbia. She lived for a long time with her husband and six children on a farm in Canada. She is a weaver and potter. One morning her husband came in and said, 'I'm off now' and left. For good. Wanja had a farm and six children to look after and was therefore very stressed by the prospect, but being a devotee of an Indian Guru called Muktanand, she had great trust in the Divine Gift. She prayed to her teacher to take care of her. Very soon she heard of a Japanese lady coming to the area to teach people healing. Wanja met Takata and a deep friendship was born. She was initiated and later became a Master before moving to British Columbia. She has taught many of the Tribal Indians Reiki and helped them regain their confidence in their history and self-worth. She, in return, has been privileged to learn from them Shamanism – American Indian healing through altered states, knowledge of non-ordinary reality, and earth remedies. Wanja has written a book called *In the Light of a Distant Star* in which she talks about Reiki, her closeness to Takata and of seeing dragons!

In the early 1980s Wanja went on a visit to India to see her Guru, Muktanand. There she was introduced to another devotee called Martha Sylvester. Martha was staying in the same Ashram and had heard of Reiki but was not going to pursue it until she returned to England. She was very surprised one day when her room mate came skipping in saying, 'You'll never believe it, there's a Reiki Master in the Ashram.' Martha was later initiated and eventually became a Master herself in 1985. In 1988 she was given permission to initiate her own Masters.

My journey to Reiki

My personal journey to Reiki began after many years investigating the metaphysical plane. At 16 I realized I was not like the other people around me. In fact I was so different that my parents sent me to a psychiatrist who sat in a rocking chair with dark glasses on and waited for half an hour for me to speak. I seriously wondered who needed treatment here! I taught myself to meditate. It came to me as a journey away from the surface madness and into a place of safe calm where everything made sense. After many years of trying to fit in to numerous peer groups and failing dismally, I learnt the Transcendental Meditation (TM) Programme of Maharishi Mahesh Yogi. This is a system of mantra meditation, and the use of sutras on a subtle level, including levitation, knowledge of other worlds, and access to cosmic consciousness. I spent at least two months of every year in the Ashrams learning the Siddhis, the Bhagavad Gita, the Rig Veda (The Book of Truth), listening only to the sound of Sama Veda (Songs of Truth, Indian Pandits chanting ancient vibrational sound to affect consciousness). I was there at the beginning of Maharishi's TM Siddhi Programme and practised diligently for seven years.

Although TM gave me a structure and a theory, in practice the experience I was looking for was still fairly random. I realized that mantra meditation was still working on the level of mind and I wanted to dive directly into Being. I became disillusioned with TM and the obsession with the technique. I didn't want to become a Hindu, I wanted peace in my heart. The TM Movement required me not to be myself but conform, not only to behaving like the others but also to wearing the same clothes – no make-up, flat sandals, etc. I wanted to be just me, a nonconformist Aquarian by birth, and so, sadly and traumatically, I gave up all my belief in The Movement. I am, however, eternally grateful to Maharishi for his wisdom and for giving me a good start.

In my search to be me and accepted as such, a friend introduced me to Prem Rawat, affectionately known as 'Maharaji', a 21-year-old Americanized Asian Brahman with a wife, four children and a dog. I was initiated into the 'Knowledge' of Maharaji in 1981. Maharaji began teaching Divine Knowledge at the age of eight and came to the West when he was 12. He gives a direct experience of God through four techniques, namely Inner Light, Inner Sound, Inner Taste and Inner Feeling. Reiki, to me, is the fifth technique – Inner Touch. I needed to give nothing except myself and a commitment to myself to maintain the connection. That connection is not dependent upon the technique, although enhanced by it. It is the ultimate relationship of Master/Student/Knowledge of God. This I practise every day and is my greatest gift.

In 1986 I gave birth to my daughter, Kim, which to me was the ultimate initiation of all, the chance to experience for the first time what Unconditional Love meant. While pregnant I began studying Rising Dragon Tai Chi Chuan and went on to learn short form, long form, mirror form and sword form Chi Gong, Push Hands, Ta Lu. Tai Chi is a martial art consisting of meditation in action and inner energy exercises. It brings about a deep understanding of Chi, energy, and the Tao of Other or way of others.

In 1990 I was 'Opened' in Subud – this is a form of spontaneous Divine Worship and cathartic purification. It comes from an Indonesian Sufi teacher called Bapak who realized that by practising his deep Divine Worship in the presence of others the energy would be transferred to them also. They would then be able to practise by themselves, even though group practice is encouraged as a support and as a more powerful process.

From time to time I investigate the way of the Shaman, having been taken through the 'Shaman's Death' by circumstance. For myself I use herbs, tinctures and remedies as well as stones and ritual, but never in my Reiki treatments. Reiki must be kept pure and simple.

I came to Reiki through my Tai Chi teacher who offered it as a way to assist our growth and understanding of ourselves. His Reiki Master was Martha, to whom I was introduced in 1988 and received First Degree. Having organized the class I joked that I would be a Master one day soon. I received Second Degree in 1988 also and began working with Martha, organizing her classes and assisting her with them. Within a year and a half I had organized the classes that were to teach 150 people. Martha was one of only about five or six Masters in the UK at that time and taught Usui Shiki Ryoho. There are now a greater number of Reiki Masters in the UK, but very few of them honour the original principles.

In 1989 I was privileged to meet Wanja when she came to Cardiff to see Martha. I arrived late and rather exhausted having just recovered from severe mumps. As it runs in my family to be early, being late was exceedingly stressful. I entered the full room rather sheepishly and hoped not to be noticed, but there was only one chair left, and that was in front of Wanja. It was my fortune. Wanja gazed into me with her endless pools of blue eyes and thereafter instructed Martha to make me a Master.

I became a Master in 1989 as I could not refuse an offer that only comes once in a lifetime, even though my life was in turmoil and change. I was about to have my second baby and separated from my husband at the same time. I began my two years of apprenticeship. I was initiated when six months' pregnant and taught my first class when nine months' pregnant. The apprenticeship was like the rock in a stormy sea. Whether I liked it or not, Reiki had to become my focus. Teaching appeared from nowhere and allowed us to move on.

I was thrown in at the deep end with the teaching, having never even stood up in front of a group before. I had to fight through my nervousness and learn to teach the hard way. Martha gave me the initiation and said, 'Let the Reiki do the talking'. What else could I do? I took many classes before I felt confident and safe teaching this subject. Today it is required that Reiki Masters study a teacher training course appropriate to the country (see Chapter 9). I did, however, learn that Reiki can take you way beyond the limitations and expectations of yourself.

I underwent the Master Teaching Training while awaiting the birth of my son, Tallis, having somehow bypassed the three years of preparation due to my background training. I rekindled my interest in drawing, painting and the art of Seeing, having spent ten years since my Art College degree course running my own, successful, men's knitwear business. I am today a practising, working artist constantly investigating ways of seeing energy through light, form, movement and pushing the barriers of the known world. Since completing a Master's Degree in Fine Art at Bath Spa University, my work has matured beyond the figurative and relies on the art of abstract automatic writing to attempt to describe the awesome presence of the sublime. I create visual poetry on a large scale, maybe two metres square, to entice people to question and look again within their own understanding. The combination of all things makes me whole, but Reiki is the first line of defence in times of stress. It gives me the means to hold the physical world still with my hands, quietening the mind, calming my emotions and allowing me to dive deeply into the place of Spirit wherein lies inherent wisdom. Reiki is so profound, it reveals your true self to you.

Since 1989 I have only taught five further teaching Masters who each trained with me for over six years. I have begun the training of several others who have not managed the commitment or decided to skip the apprenticeship and learn in one day on the cheap. Reiki chooses its own Masters. Takata did not teach anyone else for over 37 years; now some Masters boast about initiating over a thousand teaching Masters themselves. There is far more to it than meets the eye.

the nature of illness

I feel it is important to analyse and understand why we get ill in the first place. What is it that knocks us out of balance? What long-term effects does that have on our physical, mental and emotional health? If we allow ourselves to disintegrate through being stressed in the world then sooner or later the body will begin to disintegrate also.

The first line of defence is awareness and recognition of the symptoms we are carrying that can be healed. Second is to change the habits that prevent us from being healthy happy people.

Reiki is energy medicine and by its nature repairs and restores energy. We need to feel fullness rather than emptiness. Action and determination will bring about a permanent change and bring us to harmony.

Reiki falls comfortably into the category of energy medicine. Energy medicine works on the premise that consciousness directly affects constitution. It is true that illness can bring about complete transformation as it takes us on a journey from pain, discomfort and entropy to well-being by seeking assistants to help with this condition, whether they be people, herbs, tinctures, elixirs, chemicals, objects, ritual, religion or healing touch.

Stress is the modern-day causative factor in many illnesses. Stress is our inability to cope with or assimilate that which is placed upon us. When in a state of stress we may feel tense, tight, full of thoughts, restless in sleep, that we have no time, tense in personal relationships, a fear of losing control, physical discomfort, lack of enjoyment, lack of fulfilment, negative emotions, anger, irritability, we have no time to practise techniques for stress management, we need medication to suppress symptoms. The body can take only so much before its energy begins to implode and we take to our beds. The body in an imploded state perpetuates itself.

When relaxed and well we feel expanded, loose, clear thinking, rested, we have plenty of time, we have good communication in relationships, controlled without controlling, strong, flexible, enjoyment of life, fulfilment, satisfaction, optimism, we can give time to the practice of techniques and habits to keep us healthy. The body in an expansive state perpetuates itself.

Our bodies are created from the combined energies of our soul-self, emotional-self and mind-self and the relationship of all these levels to the Spirit Energy or Universal Divine Energy. They are a reflection of our inner condition. We are not our bodies but our bodies are us.

To explain this further I would first like to describe these areas of Being as separate aspects with separate unique qualities.

From spirit into being – a summary

Spirit is infinite energy, it is everywhere. It has no boundaries but can become manifest.

Soul is a condensation of spirit. It is personal. It is also infinite, when healthy, and has no boundaries, yet it belongs. It is spirit focused.

Emotion is a condensation of soul. It is totally personal and subjective. It responds to the interaction of external forces with itself. It is connected to soul via the heart.

Mind is a condensation of emotion. It is dense, yet unseen, and takes on qualities of the earth plane, such as duality.

Body is a condensation of all other levels of being. Its density allows it to manifest as sensory substance. The bones are so dense that they do not easily decay. They contain the history of our ancestors. The body is a mirror of the well-being of soul, emotion and mind.

The nature of the soul

The soul is the subtlest part of our energy system. It is in direct union with the Spirit Energy and is formed from its substance by grace, love and intent. The soul is the part of us that we are constantly looking for and constantly longing for. That is to say, a place of balance on the level of emotion. We feel our soul very deeply when we are in love, yet we cannot find even a glimpse of it when we are in distress. Various experiences in life remind us that it is there, or maybe that it no longer feels that it is there. Sometimes we get so depressed that we feel we have lost our soul. This is because, in part, we have.

When we suffer deep trauma, loss, accident or invasion, the part of our soul-self that governs that emotion will separate not only from Spirit, but also from our body. As more parts of the soul separate, the being becomes vulnerable and weakened, attracting to it more imbalance with less resistance. As whatever happens on the energetic level also happens simultaneously to the physical, it is easy to see that disease can be caused by a weakening of the energy structure long before it manifests in the body as pain or discomfort.

The soul can only be repaired by us becoming conscious of it and using life's experiences as a mirror from which to see ways of becoming strong instead of weak, empowered instead of vulnerable. It needs to be reintegrated on each level of being and cannot be dealt with by itself. The mindset has to change to allow the level of self-esteem, self-worth and self-knowledge to be strong enough; emotion needs to be clear of impulsive, obsessive patterns and the body needs to be able to regenerate its light content for the integration to be permanent. As Reiki addresses all levels simultaneously this process can happen quite rapidly. So as we heal the subtle body (that is, the energy body), changes will eventually occur in the physical body as afterwaves, then harmony returns.

What does the soul feel like? You may know more about the nature of soul when you feel you have lost it than when it is comfortable inside you. Then you will recognize it when it comes home and becomes whole.

The nature of the emotions

Emotion is the bridge between the soul and the manifest being. It is the gauge with which we feel when we have strayed from the path of our heart. Emotion is a spontaneous reaction to the external world yet is coloured by past experience. It creates a physical response, a sensation or sensations that can be felt in the body, observed and subsequently acted upon. The gateway to integrating spirit and soul with mind and body is emotion. The heart is at the centre of the spectrum and is the seat of love. It is only when the heart is healed that we feel whole. Only then can we live with love in our lives. Our inherent nature and our past experiences determine our feelings, yet it is how we nurture those feelings that allows us to heal. By allowing the voices and our listening skills to descend from the mind into the heart, wisdom can be heard in the sensations of feeling, and knowledge of how to act becomes clear.

It has become clear to me in the twenty years of being a therapist that the main emotions that perpetuate a lack of wellbeing are loss, grief and the subsequent emptiness. Each contains the other in some way.

We first experience loss in childhood as something that is taken away from or something we need that is never given. This may be material, such as a toy or food, or it may be the withholding of or lack of love. The loss is continual throughout life and cannot be avoided and each subsequent time we feel it, it adds to the past experience, growing inside us.

Loss can also be experienced in its external form as grief, another emotion that is unavoidable and out of our control. Grief creates a deep wound that takes its own time to heal and keeps returning like the tide. It can lead to depression, energy depleting illnesses and suicidal feelings. Anger is also a common symptom of grief as the mind tries to reason with the pain of this strong emotion. Depression is merely the other face of anger and both contain tremendous forces of energy that need to be tapped and utilized in creative ways in order to progress life instead of creating illness.

Loss, grief and emptiness cause deep levels of stress, especially as the heart and soul become separated by the traumas. We are often surprised when everything seems fine until something triggers the memory of that loss and then we fall apart.

Reiki can act as a balancing tool to return us to a calm and centred place from where we can look out at our pain, anger or depression and begin to understand that they are natural and valid emotions. Then, logically and rationally, we can work it all out. In the case of emptiness we can find that rather than dull and fearful the feeling of nothingness can become meditative, alive and full of potential. Above all the more we fight the feelings the more they will persist. We let go only when we can replace the stress with calm and reason with ourselves that this is all part of life.

The nature of the mind

The mind governs our actions, it instructs the body and emotions on the basis of its reflective experience of the external world. The reflection it sees is from a unique perspective of the personality of that particular person. The reality we choose to believe in at any given moment is the outside world seen through the veil of our past experiences and emotions, coloured also by what we choose to believe in order to be part of our peer structure and society.

The mind by its very nature is dualistic; black/white, this/that, up/down, here/there, existence/non-existence, happy/sad. Therefore it is easy to have one set of beliefs one day and to find out that tomorrow the opposite is true. Which one is true, then, if our mind can talk us into and out of both sides quite logically and rationally? Both are possible truths but neither are the ultimate truth, for that place resides in the still point in the centre of mind where consciousness becomes conscious of itself and remains neutral in all argument as it knows all things are of equal value in the realm of experience.

It is the veering from positive thought to negative thought that holds the body out of balance. When the emotions are triggered by the attraction of the outside world our mind creates a judgement on the validity of the experience and triggers off a chemical change in the body according to the emotion. If it decides the attraction is a good and joyful experience it will produce chemicals that expand the energy system, and create reactions in the brain and nervous system that make the body feel good. If it decides the attraction is fearful it will create a chemical reaction that stimulates tension in the body, discomfort in the solar plexus and a shrinking of the energy system. The mind can alter the body instantly and consequently plays a very big part in its healing. Healing is not just about the wound in the body; it is the wounded attitude that really feeds the fire.

Only you can know your thoughts, only you can tame the mind and choose which thoughts to discard. First, get to know your mind then teach it to cease, then you will know the meaning of repose.

When the mind is agitated there is a corresponding tension somewhere in the body and likewise, if the body is tense, there will be a corresponding agitation in the mind. So to withdraw the mind from that which excites and agitates we must first settle the body. When we still the body and allow its functions to relax, expand and quieten, then the mind can begin to follow down into a deep place of stillness, beyond which lies the level of consciousness we call transcendence. That is, a place of Being beyond the mind, or in truth, it is a place of stillness before the mind begins. It is not the empty screen onto which all images can be projected, but the light which allows the image to become visible. This place can be experienced through Reiki treatment as the body is given permission to be held still and the mind is also held still with the physical hands. Intent creates the form. Attention creates the experience. Thought is not predestined, it is a reaction to the impressions which are received in the present, thus it can be directed for benefit only if we stay alert. We begin with a state of excitation, gain control from within by learning to hold the mind still and gain perception of the true nature of Spirit.

To treat the symptoms of the body with chemicals, or to treat the symptoms of the mind with therapy are in themselves not enough, for the whole instrument must be retuned. Reiki initiation attunes the human instrument to a direct pathway from the grossest form, the body, to the subtlest form, the Spirit, by allowing us to bypass normal thinking through its meditative quality, bringing about profound change.

The mind is very powerful, it can create images, words, ideas and concepts, it can change chemicals and choose its own destiny, it can even trick its own master. What must be remembered, however, is that it is not just a random alien that has been transplanted into our head but it is a reflection of our being and the integration (or disintegration) of the aspects that make us whole. The mind is a part of the instrument that we have created from our conscious will to exist. Now we must get it under control and put it in its place. It is our servant; we are not its slave.

The nature of the body

As we have already seen, the body is a physical manifestation of all other aspects of ourselves. It is an electromagnetic generator. It is energy vibrating, just as the other aspects are, yet it is far more dense than those parts we cannot see with the physical eye. Anatomy and physiology are incomplete in terms of whole-view theory, for the energetic is a system in itself that enables the anatomy and physiology to communicate.

Our subtle bodies are constantly being influenced by the environment as well as by our personality, the atmosphere, electromagnetism of the Earth, weather, climate, seasons, months and hours. Even the aspects of the planets at the moment we are born influence our individuality, and the Moon has a hold over our emotions.

We form our inner environment, our constitution, from the air, water, minerals, plant and animal life that we ingest, together with their corresponding electromagnetic vibrations. The balance between our external and internal environment creates our physical and mental planes. It is an interaction, a participation with our environment. The external has infinite dimension while the internal is limited by our physical boundaries, it is more dense and compact yet also subject to change. The incoming and outgoing energy must balance or there will be overexpansion or degeneration. Our basic constitution is created by our inherited genetic patterning and by our mother's diet before we were born, as well as her physical and mental attitude during gestation. Constitutional change is slow, expanding and contracting like a breath, while the external conditions change rapidly, being influenced by all other things that are in motion.

As we evolve we become more sensitive to the subtle energies and become affected by those outside fields that influence our own body. We begin to notice the effects of electromagnetic pollution from televisions, computers, low-dose plugs switched on, domestic machinery, light bulbs, cars, transmitters, general static and even satellite interference.

Reiki can affect all physical symptoms, pain relief being the most obvious. It has also been found that the skeleton realigns into balance during treatment; the cells enliven and begin to throw off disease; blood pressure can balance from high or low to more normal; diabetics find they need less insulin. When people are under severe stress, suffer from depression or insomnia, they find that they can cope better without the need for medication. Colds, flu and general infections can clear more rapidly. In cases of injury, tissue damage heals well and broken bones mend fast and strong.

As the physiology awakens, the dis-ease lessens. Of course, other factors are also important to observe such as diet, water, air, exercise, mental attitude, but to start with a hands-on practical experience that has immediate benefit is the best place for a kick start, especially to the doubting mind.

the nature of health

So we have looked at what knocks us out of balance and now we look at how to restore health and wellbeing.

Subtle changes in life habits bring about profound changes in all aspects of our physical, mental and emotional selves.

We need to create an action plan of change and have a willingness to let go of those old habits in order to encourage the changes to be effective. The food on your plate is the body of tomorrow and as such must be viewed as the best medicine. Air, exercise, water, light, food and positive thinking will eventually combine to bring back happiness as a state of being.

We can have a long-term goal but need to work one day at a time. Detrimental habits will only go when they are replaced with those that nurture.

If illness is dysfunction (disintegration), then health is natural function (integration). To take control of our own health and maintain it as we swim through the sea of experiences without sinking, awareness must awaken and focus be kept.

Breath and exercise

The Breath is the key to all of the mysteries.

Joseph Rael, *Being and Vibration*

Breath is vital, it is our vitality. Breath, or Prana as it is known in Indian Yoga systems, is the vehicle for Divine Knowledge. Oxygen is its messenger. We are fortunate that breathing does itself as otherwise we would forget. It is our first contact with the world when we become independent from our mother host. It is our introduction to our relationship with the Divine Will. A yogi measures his life in numbers of breaths rather than numbers of years. Thus stressed, rapid, shallow breathing causes early demise whereas complete, conscious, purifying breath causes longevity. In India, breath is taught as a science called pranayama. It is through controlled conscious activity of the breath that different states of being are obtained and different states of health ensue.

Exercise in a fresh, pollution-free atmosphere is the quickest way to revitalize energy to a depleted system. Exercise itself helps to free toxins which may be eliminated more rapidly as the metabolism speeds up. It also increases the dimensions of the lungs, allowing the full breath to have greater capacity. Stamina and endurance come about through less effort. The resting state of the lungs creates deeper oxygenation. Exercise turns the inertia and entropy into substance of useful density such as muscles and bones – the storehouses of power and motion. Exercise also strengthens the function of organs and boosts the immune system. The exercise machines at my gymnasium chant 'strong body, strong mind'. Twenty minutes per day in fresh air is recommended for maintaining general health.

Reiki self-treatment on the heart and solar plexus positions creates a focus on the breath in a position of restful alertness.

We can then become conscious. During the restfulness of treatment, the breath naturally becomes slower and more full. Vitality then enters the cells as they open up to receive. A natural state of balance returns and is usually felt as peaceful joy or bliss. Bliss is a lovely word that does not describe an emotion but a state of being. When the bliss state is reached it is a recognition of the fulfilment of longing.

Water

A large percentage of the body is water, yet we habitually replace it with tea/coffee/cola/sugary drinks. Water is the container of messages. It is the vehicle for electricity and healthy function of not only physical cells but the fluids that move around the body and the emotions that govern the instrument. When we drink energized water such as natural spring or mineral water, our energy fields lighten and expand.

Fresh spring water has more vitality than tap water. Tap water has more vitality than boiled water or water containing any other substance. When other substances dissolve in water it ceases to be the power of itself and takes on the messages of the contained chemical substances. Coffee is toxic and therefore the whole cup including the water is contaminated with toxic messages.

Water is vital for cleansing, detoxifying and eliminating other substances. It is filtered through the kidneys (the seat of all emotion, grief and tears). Whenever Reiki is applied to the body, toxin release is increased so water becomes a prerequisite to help flush these away. It is the burden of toxins that weakens the system and thereby their elimination through treatment that brings back its strength. Water is the element of healthy bodily function and release. Water is vital for the healthy function of the processes of urination, sweating, out breath, tears, salivation – the processes of purification. When the vehicle is distorted by contamination then the messages are not clearly sent through the nervous system. Just a sip of water, or even the visualization of being in water, will restore electrical balance and reduce the fatigue of stress.

Light

Light is the source of all energy on Earth – it is absorbed by plants which are then eaten by animals, it is transposed during biological and chemical changes within organisms into other forms of vibration. Fundamentally all things require an influx of energy to remain in existence. With light we can see clearly, we are warmed, we are fed. Light affects the brain chemistry to produce the sense of happiness. In countries where the days are short people often suffer from an illness called SAD – Seasonal Affective Disorder: the remedy is daylight. Daylight can turn around depression, anxiety and grief. When holiday time comes there is a mass exodus to the nearest beach where we can bask in the sun and recharge our tired, worn batteries.

Reiki is light in motion; it can be seen by some as colours pouring out through the hands affecting the light colours of the body. That is why we feel so marvellous during and after treatment. Our hearts are lightened, our minds are cleared and the body's heaviness disappears. When we lighten up we are happy.

Food

We can change to a lighter, fresher, more varied diet that contains direct life force. Energy from the Sun is stored in plant cells together with elements of the Earth that create the vitamins and minerals we need to create our own complex organism. If we eat fresh, raw or lightly cooked food, we take in the liveliest source of energy. We need less food as all we eat contains vitality. The tendency in the Western diet is to overeat, especially dairy products and refined carbohydrates. It is a misinterpretation of the body's calling for more energy. It is not calling for more food but simply more energy. So a smaller quantity of higher vitality food will satisfy the body, keep the structure strong, produce less waste and stagnation and reflect on the mental and emotional well-being also. Processed food, refined carbohydrate, sugars, pre-cooked, frozen or microwaved foods all contain depleted life force.

Kirlian photography of refined, processed food shows very little life force at all, so you can see why the body craves so much of it. Hence the obvious high rate of illness in the fast food era when we are all too busy to wash our own vegetables. A quick burger and chips washed down with cola contains hardly a trace of vitality. It contains bulk but does not feed or regenerate the breakdown of tissues.

A living energetic system must be fed with fresh living energy, otherwise entropy and inertia move in. The mind becomes dull and depressed, and life feels like pushing treacle up hill. We are so saturated with sugar and acid-forming foods that the electrical currents no longer provide an open frequency of communication from which conscious experience is gained. It has become a vicious circle.

It is no coincidence that most Indian sages and modern-day gurus eat a vegetarian diet consisting mostly of whole grain, fruit, vegetables, vegetable protein, a small amount of fat and little sugar or dairy. It is not part of a fad but becomes an essential refinement of consciousness. Gradually, as Reiki works on the system, it is possible to give up the need for stimulants such as tea, coffee and alcohol, the density of meat and dairy, and the heaviness of processed food. It doesn't mean that everyone must be vegetarian or that if you drink coffee and eat meat you cannot be either well or enlightened because it is down to the basics of consciousness on the level of being. An Eskimo would find it a big problem being vegetarian but that doesn't exclude him or her from the experience of peace, health, love and happiness. Come as you are and see what you may become.

Rest

Rest – wakeful, conscious rest – is as important as sleep; meditation, resting the mind, relaxation of the body and being still without distraction on the surface. Rest to music is good yet rest in stillness is best. Reiki self-treatment is the perfect tool and perfect excuse to be still. The regeneration is far more subtle when in wakeful rest than in the rest of sleep. It is a chance to listen to the body.

There are states of restful balance in the body that are natural and normal. The body will return to these inherent states once stress and tension are no longer the main force. This relates not only to the structure of the body but also to the constitution.

During illness the structure of the body contracts, becoming vulnerable and weak. The organs become congested, the lungs cannot fill fully, the intestines become stagnant and general vitality diminishes. The pressure of blood increases as it struggles to complete its cycle without freedom of energy. Mental balance also moves away from natural rest and clarity.

The body's natural balance of wisdom cannot be maintained with drugs, it has to have awareness. Posture is an integral part of the body's health. The well person is upright, expansive and relaxed with resting energy at the ready to become thoughts, actions, movements, etc. The sick body constricts all natural capacity for freedom. Through Reiki treatment the deep relaxation addresses all levels of structure – muscles, tendons, ligaments, cells and bones – opening and inviting the remembering of a state of being unfamiliar to modern man. Harmony can only be rekindled in balanced rest.

Love

Love is the most powerful and beautiful of human qualities without which we can feel isolated, alone and sometimes we can even die from the lack of it. Children who are neglected and unloved by their parents become weak or aggressive and may develop mental, emotional and behavioural disorders.

It is our birthright to one day find happiness and enduring love. Love is the affirmation of our connection to the world.

Many people are ill through, not only the lack of being loved but also the lack of being able to feel the sensation of love for others.

Love feeds the heart and reconnects it to the soul. Personal love gives the sensation of belonging, of purpose and attachment. Love given out is returned in the joy of giving. Unconditional love is the strongest bond we have with another person – the love of a parent for a child or the child for the parent. Starved of love we either turn inwards and become unbalanced or turn outwards towards violence and hatred. In either case, happiness then becomes hard to acquire.

Reiki is the purest, simplest force of energy that can be seen as light and felt as love. It is this quality of love, and that is the universal love, that enables it to heal by integrating all forms of energy. During a treatment the connection is made between one being and another in a bond of honesty and caring yet without being about the personality of for any particular goal other than to feel what is happening in the present moment, for that is the only thing that is real.

People sometimes describe the treatment as feeling like being held gently in the arms of the mother. Practise daily self-treatment and begin to regain the love for yourself that takes away all loneliness and makes you feel fulfilled.

Personal love is concentrated universal love. It manifests as love for family, friends and, especially, love for one's partner. This kind of love creates a precious personal bond that heals the deepest of hurt.

Love is not as essential as food and water for survival but for human happiness it is key.

5

initiation

Initiation is the essence of Reiki practice. It is what differentiates Reiki from other forms of therapy and is the first step towards self-knowledge. It activates the universal energy so we can begin to see it in everyday life. Anyone can receive the unique attunements that allow Reiki to flow freely through each person regardless of previous knowledge or ability.

Reiki is invisible but can begin to be felt as heat or tingling in the hands as it moves through the giver into the recipient.

The initiation process is performed one to one before the Reiki hand positions are learnt and applied to both oneself and others. It comes as an unlimited supply of energy to top up the depleted person.

Reiki is not only the transmission of energy but also the transference of knowledge. Not information, but the knowledge of the heart, knowledge of the creator. The transmission is done by invocation, but the transference is made by the Master's own knowledge of the Divine and by their ability to be directly connected to the Reiki within them as the initiation takes place. Another reason to choose wisely in your teacher.

Preparation of the Master is as essential as that of the student. The technique for transmission is simple and easy to learn. It involves the Usui symbols to call forth and activate the various levels of consciousness to which they pertain. They are keys to unlock energy of a particular vibration that is utilized in a specific way, enabling the Reiki to be accessed, unhindered by the personality of the giver. The Master needs to prepare by returning to the state of creative consciousness available only through dedication and devotional practice. The Master may appear to be sitting still and at times doing nothing, but in the doing nothing a vast field of energy is being held for you to contact. At the point of teaching, the Master must have more energy than the student in order to lift them up into the experience of Divine Knowledge. Just giving information of a technique does not suffice.

The initiations are the essential part of the Form, the difference between Reiki and all other forms of healing. They allow the pathway of energy to be drawn down through the top of the head, through the heart, into the solar plexus and out through the hands. They alter the vibrational flow of the body and align it in such a way as to gain permanent access to the source of all things. I use the analogy of a hose pipe turned on but with a kink in it. The Master has been trained to find the kink and undo it so the water can flow freely once again. It is really nothing new, only a remembering.

Entrainment

During attunement, a change takes place within the student by a scientific process known as 'entrainment'. Entrainment is when two oscillating electromagnetic systems come into each other's proximity, each operating at its own frequency, or vibration. Both frequencies change resonation to become synchronized with the other, the lower lifting towards the higher. In this way, the energy that emanates from the Master at the time of initiation engages the energy of the student in the process of that entrainment. This electromagnetic resonance settles at the higher frequency that is most natural to it, which is why we feel better. This is also found to be the dominant process during the treatment. The energy of the practitioner aligns with that of the receiver, the two pulse as one, the energy of the receiver raises itself by following the resonance. The advanced Reiki techniques give the practitioner tools to activate the electromagnetism in the hands and the ability to be more conscious of this experience. Even the breath can become naturally co-ordinated and as one is breathing out, the other is breathing in. This assists the balance and unity and creates the clarity needed for the healing to take place.

The form of First Degree initiation

During the initiation the student agrees to receive and the Master is in a state to give. The exchange is made to create the gateway for return. There are four initiations for First Degree. The first aligns the crown, the second the heart, the third the solar plexus and the fourth seals the pathway through the hands. From the first session the energy begins to flow. Many people ask what happens during the initiation as we ask them to close their eyes.

The initiations begin with the student seated and the Master behind in preparation. The Master first makes conscious contact with the pure Reiki and focuses the intent. The Master bows, in gratitude, to the Reiki Masters in their lineage as a sign of respect for the gift; they bow to the student as a sign of service and respect for the student. The first invocation begins over the crown to call upon the energy to align in this way. Several of the sacred symbols are used at this point to unlock the energy vibration. With one hand over the crown a silent invocation is made to call upon the Divine White Light to enter. Once this is activated the hand is placed on the head and the invocation continues. The Master then comes to the front of the student and clasps their hands in a posture for the invocation of Divine Light to come through the hands. The hands are lifted above the brow and a Holy Breath is formed to blow a cleansing breath on the hands, brow and crown. A Holy Breath is given to the heart and solar plexus also.

The hand clasp is sealed with a further invocation as the energy begins to enter the hands. The Master passes behind the student again and, using an empowerment posture and gesture with the hands, blesses the student and bows in gratitude. A clap brings the student into the present.

The second and third initiations follow the above pattern and include invocation via the hands of the Master on the shoulders of the student, energizing the throat and heart chakras. The fourth initiation follows the same path as the first but after the crown has been energized, the Master's hands gently cup the head as an invocation is made to seal the new experience.

The purpose of four sessions is a gradual alignment interspersed with grounding by practical experience, questioning and knowledge-giving sessions.

Sometimes nothing seems to be felt at all during this profound and powerful process and the student looks up in amazement with an 'Is that it?' question in their eyes. Other times, warmth and tingling can be felt. Some people have wonderful visions, or symbolic colours appear. Some like the place so much that they almost refuse to return, so I clap loudly at the end! Experience is as varied as the diversity of people. The initiations are performed one to one in silence. Sometimes the second, third and fourth can be undertaken in small groups but no more than three at a time. The Master must not interfere with the process with ego as may happen in a large group.

The moment of initiation brings about union with Reiki – union with the Divine – and needs respect. It is a ritual of invocation and direction of Divine Light, a holy act of purification. The initiation in itself will transform as it changes the essential vibrational frequency of the student. The frequency with which the soul-self of the student operates is raised so that what is put out is in balance and harmony, therefore what comes back in circumstance and relationship is also in balance and harmony.

Once the full initiation has taken place, this alignment remains eternally. It is possible, however, to focus on the mind, the emotions and the negativity of the world and thereby mask the openness to God. But it will still be there waiting for you to return with your effort and practice.

First Degree Reiki part one: self-treatment

The starting point once the initiations have taken place is to treat oneself. The physical postures taught in a class are simple, practical and cover the whole body. In my teaching I hope to give confidence to the student to practise at home and focus on the stillness within. Daily self-treatment can be practised from as little as five minutes up to half an hour and it is the enjoyment of the feeling of it that encourages us to go on. Through regular treatment all physical tensions, mental agitation and stress will begin to subside and be replaced with energy, confidence and well-being. So we gain the strength and capability to look after our own health in the world. When we relax we become happy and when we become happy we can radiate love and kindness.

It must be stressed that self-treatment is the most important aspect of Reiki. To treat others allows us to give and feel a sense of purpose, but to be able to address our own pain, suffering and difficulties is self-empowering. It is not until we refer back to our own attitude with a view to change that we can look out compassionately to the world of others.

Decide how much time to put aside for self-treatment. Half an hour a day is recommended for a steady and comfortable transformation to take place, but to begin with it is whatever you will allow yourself. Many people find that before bedtime or first thing in the morning are the easiest times to put aside. Self-treatment is best performed lying down as the arms are held by gravity and don't ache as they do when sitting upright.

The initiation must first be undertaken and energy exchanged for the transmission of awareness to begin to flow.

Find a quiet place where you will not be disturbed. Turn off the telephone, put out the cat and be sure your children are occupied. Treat this time as precious – the time you have always been waiting for among the noise, the hustle and bustle, the demands and stresses of the day. It is best not to play relaxing music as this will only entertain the mind and distract it from entering deep within.

Lie down with feet uncrossed and begin with a couple of minutes to bring the awareness to the present. Remind yourself that for this session the worries and tensions are not needed. Let the hands become Listening Hands. Keep the fingers relaxed yet together so that the hand and fingers act as one complete unit.

As you place the hands on each position, all that is required is that you firstly observe the mind chatter and secondly, allow it to quieten. It is also best to allow the body to settle into each position for a minute first so that the implantation is on a deep and subtle level.

The form of self-treatment

Position 1: Place the hands over the eyes

Position 2: Place the hands over the top of the head

Position 3: Place the hands around the jaw including the jaw muscle

Position 4: The hands tuck underneath the head

Position 5: Cup the ears

Position 6: Place the hands over the throat

Position 7: The heart and solar plexus

Position 8: The lower abdomen

Position 9: The genitals

Position 10: The knees

Position 11: The ankles and feet

Self-treatment – the finishing-off technique

The purpose of this part of the form is to give the deeply relaxed body a sense of its boundary once more and to stimulate the surface body to awaken without the sense of deep relaxation being taken away.

1 Rotate the ankle both ways to its limit.

2 Massage the toes and foot deeply with the thumbs.

3 With both hands, squeeze up the leg three times from the ankle to the hip.

4 Again with both hands, stroke the leg in an energetic upward motion and seep off at the top.

5 Repeat with the other leg.

6 Massage the hand.

7 Squeeze up the arm including the shoulder muscle.

8 Stroke up the arm and sweep off at the top, as with the leg.

9 Repeat with the other hand.

10 'Gallop' the fingers in a tapping motion on the skull to enliven the brain.

11 Massage the ears, holding the lobes at the end.

12 Tap the centre of the chest three times to wake up the immune system.

13 Cross the hands over the chest to give thanks.

14 Rest for a few minutes before getting up.

7

First Degree Reiki part two: treatment of others

The second part of Reiki First Degree teaches the full treatment covering the whole body and therefore addressing all problems within, whatever the source and without the need for knowledge of anatomy or physiology.

Reiki is not learnt with the mind but is an experience. It is a non-invasive technique in which the body is held very still and the person is allowed to dip deeply into the place of quiet calm that is so restorative. The treatment is still but is completed with an awakening technique that is both invigorating and grounding.

Self-treatment, as in the previous chapter, can be practised without initiation to some good effect but it is important to receive proper training before practising on others.

Reiki in practice – the Listening Hands technique

The learning environment must support the aspect of purity and simplicity first and foremost with nothing added from other disciplines. No New Age music, no gongs or chants, no clearing of stuff. It must contain only Reiki if anyone is to know what they are receiving. It must not be diluted with other ideas or dogmas, crystals, rattles or drums. These have a sacred place also but they are not appropriate here. It is for the Master, the Reiki and the student alone, for the student can experience what Reiki is only when they quieten the clutter of the mind and go within.

It is a unique way of learning. Most classes are taught with notebooks and pens. They are structured and much information is given out to be re-read at a later date as revision and reminders. Reiki is not learnt with the mind, it is a full experience and therefore cannot be forgotten. The initiations implant the connection within you like putting up a radio aerial and tuning it in to a particular frequency.

A class is usually set out in four sessions with one initiation at the beginning of each session to allow the alignment to be gradual, with a practical grounding session in between. Generally anyone who is more than 12 weeks' pregnant will be asked to return for the initiations in about a year, as once the foetus is fully formed it is felt that it is being initiated also but without personal permission. It is, however, totally safe to learn, give and receive Reiki during pregnancy. It can greatly relieve the side-effects such as nausea and backache, and is wonderful during labour to replenish energy levels between contractions and to prevent trauma.

It is important for the initiating Master to be aware of any medication being taken, especially if the student is undergoing, or has undergone in the past, treatment for depression or mental illness or suffers from any phobia or eating disorder. Drug and alcohol dependents will be given treatments rather than training until such time as they can begin the changes to be well. They are not ruled out but caution must be respected. Reiki sensitizes some people and care must be taken of them.

It must be noted that Reiki cannot be used for negative intent such as black magic or power over others as it always brings light and balance into being. Darkness cannot be empowered by light.

The energy exchange is made as people prepare to enter the first initiation. Once initiated, the energy begins to come through. All four First Degree initiations are necessary for the transmission to be complete. These may be condensed but nothing must be left out.

The ideal position in which to treat others is for them to lie down, fully clothed, with the shoes removed. This way they can reach a deep state of relaxation. Some people like to talk throughout a treatment in order not to face their fears but for most, eyes closed, in quietness, is best. Talking does not detract from the power of the Reiki but will detract from your experience of it.

It is possible to treat the whole body in a seated position which may be more appropriate for some elderly, pregnant, handicapped or disabled people or those who are sceptical and need gentle introduction. It must also be remembered that many people have fears about being touched. They may have deep-seated sexual issues or have suffered abuse. So, whatever is the most comfortable for the client will create the best results. For practitioners and those with Second Degree it is necessary to take a short case history, but for all others it is enough to ask about the structure of the body, for example, do they suffer any back pain, in order to help them be comfortable. If this is the case, a pillow under the knees will take strain off the lower back and one under the head will ease neck discomfort.

For the comfort and respect of the receiver, the practitioner should wash their hands before and after treatment. They should also clean their teeth and pay attention to personal hygiene.

Strong perfumes should be avoided and garlic should not be eaten for up to 24 hours before a treatment. How can the receiver relax if the practitioner smells strongly? The positions keep both parties close and, although absolutely no intimate personal positions are used, it is still an intimate situation. The receiver may be apprehensive.

Firstly, stand and relax, tail tucked in, head up, knees unlocked, breath relaxed and gentle. You are there for the receiver. You are privileged to be witness and facilitator.

It has been found that Reiki treatment can realign the spine, the pelvis and release traumatized muscles, tendons and ligaments. It can revitalize lesions, creating new pathways of energy to awaken nervous systems. No manipulation is necessary for this; just follow the simple non-invasive hands-on postures. Reiki allows the body to realign itself by giving it the opportunity and holding it there when it changes. Emotional trauma causes a physical trauma through the closing down of the various plexuses concerned.

The head and heart positions are the most important, but a whole body treatment is most beneficial to finding the root cause. It is not necessary to remove any clothing except shoes and glasses. The treatment is a very personal internal act and this aspect must be respected at all times, therefore no intimate positions are to be included and there is no invasion of privacy. It is possible to have very cold hands but for the receiver to experience burning heat, as what they feel is not body temperature but the transference of energy as it is drawn through.

The form of treatment of others

The head and heart positions

The treatment begins with the preparation of the giver and a gentle introduction of the two bodies to gain a sense of confidence and trust. This is done with a non-invasive and gentle stroking of the forehead and hair, allowing the mind to begin to relax.

Each position over the major organs may be held for about two minutes. This allows the energy time to begin being drawn and the cells to release.

Position 1

Position 2

Position 3

Position 4

Position 5

Position 6

Position 7

Position 8

The front positions

Position 9

Position 10

Position 11

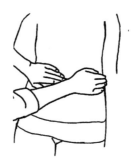

Position 12a

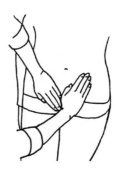

Position 12b

Position 13

Position 14

Position 15

Position 16

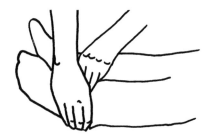

The back positions
Position 17

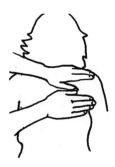

Position 18

Position 19

Position 20

Position 21

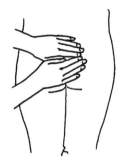

Position 22

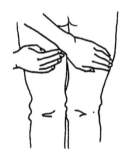

Position 23

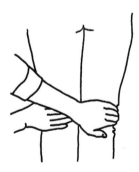

heal your life with Reiki

Position 24

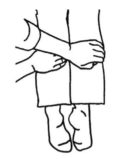

Position 25

Position 26

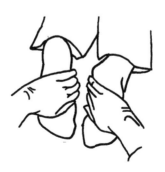

These positions constitute the treatment. They are like being allowed to lie and rest in a warm bath. The finishing-off technique is an awakening, like having an invigorating shower, but is done slowly so that the receiver comes back into the boundaries of the body, if they may have floated off, and slowly returns to their centre and back into the room in the present moment. You do not want to disturb the feeling of relaxation but you must bring them to a state of wakefulness that allows them to travel home safely, feeling good. You do not need to focus on the content of their journey unless they wish to do so as the assimilation of what has changed may take several days or even weeks to comprehend. It is a private and internal process. Pain and emotion may be released during the treatment in the form of crying and changes in the breathing patterns or it may be several days before the effects begin to show.

Treatment of others – the finishing-off technique

The technique is unique to this system and is a vital part of the grounding process and integration of the energetic with the physical.

1 Lift one foot.
2 Rotate the ankle.
3 Put the foot down to give it a firm rub with the thumbs. Standing from the body side gives access for the thumbs to work down towards the toes and include the toes.
4 Using the whole hand, lay the palms on the leg and gently squeeze in to take up the slack. It is just the point where there begins to be a resistance. Continue up the leg in, maybe, three places. Repeat twice more, making three times altogether.
5 Hold the ankle with the lower hand and with the palm of the other sweep up the surface of the leg, as if you were stroking hairs, then continue to follow through with the sweep at the end. It is like playing tennis or golf. The energy, Chi or power comes from the follow-through. Do this three times upwards towards the heart. This enlivens the tissues, gives back the sense of boundary of the body and brings the energy into the centre.

6 Repeat with the other leg.

7 Do the same with the arms. Hold their hand in your hand. Place the other hand for a few minutes on the centre of the back, then the shoulder, then the elbow and the wrist. Release the wrist, massage the palm and fingers. Standing beside the receiver, link your hand in theirs for support, squeeze up the arm and include the shoulder. Squeeze up the arms three times.

8 Stroke up the arm and flick off at the top with a follow-through sweep. Do this three times.

9 Repeat with the other arm.

10 Stand beside the body and place one hand at the top of the spine. With the other hand sweep down either side of the spine three times, but not directly on it. This should be done very gently and should not cause any shaking in the body.

11 Rub the back in a circular motion and finish with one hand over the heart centre and one on the lower spine to give the body the message to remain calm, relaxed and still. Do not 'stroke the aura' or 'fluff it up' as this interferes with the natural balance that is settling into place. The aura must remain calm and still and will change of its own accord when the body becomes balanced.

12 Take one hand off and then the other, to avoid the feeling of abandonment in the receiver. Cross them across your chest (see Figure 7.1) or put them together and give thanks to Reiki. Say three times, 'Thank you for this healing'. Then quietly, with a hand on the receiver's shoulders say, 'The treatment is now finished, you can get up when you are ready.'

Help the person up from the bed or bench, and rub their shoulders gently but vigorously to bring them back if they are still a bit floaty. Offer water to drink.

Figure 7.1 *Giving thanks position.*

Second Degree Reiki

This part of the training deals with an advanced technique that allows the process of healing at a distance. This level is undertaken after practice of the First Degree has been well established and understood. Symbols are given to the student that concentrate the energy and focus it on specific areas such as individuals, situations, and even the balance of relationships.

Second Degree is the prerequisite to practitioner training but can be used by anyone with the desire to help others and gain a deeper knowledge of the subject. It explains how thoughts manifest and gives the experience of energy being one force, wherever it is.

When we can harness this powerful force and direct it towards specific things, we have the ability to alter our lives profoundly.

In-depth and distant healing

Second Degree is known as 'the practitioner level'. It is essential training for anyone wishing to practise Reiki as a profession, although that is not what it was originally for. The prerequisite for Second Degree is at least three months' practice of First Degree on self and others. For those people who are learning Reiki solely for their own well-being, self-treatment is sufficient, but some appreciation and understanding of the power, depth and magnitude of the system is needed and can only come from the experience through practice. This level calls to an individual when they are ready for it. Reiki is the guide.

Second Degree also entails an initiation transmission, during which the three Usui symbols and mantras are given. This must be taken with a qualified, registered Master. The application of the symbols is also given at initiation. My personal undertaking as a Master of Usui Shiki Ryoho is to keep the teaching of Reiki sacred. I am unable to reveal the symbols here as they must be transmitted along with their energy essence at initiation. They can be found in books but will not unlock the Divine at the depth to which pure consciousness is activated. Beware of attempting self-initiation, as is suggested in some books, as it can unlock energies that you may not require. There is that fine line between spiritual awakening and true madness.

It is best to receive knowledge information, i.e. the symbols and their uses, some days before the initiation in order to learn and become familiar with them. This makes their application smoother and the understanding easier.

Sacred symbols

Ancient societies had no written word. Their knowledge, tribal rule of conduct and Divine Connection was passed on in oral tradition through the transmission during ritual, myths, songs, stories, visual images and sacred symbols. In ancient Egypt, the written word was considered an holy act. The writing and carving of symbols in tombs were not merely for storytelling, mythology or historical documentation, but for empowerment of the energy of the Ka or spirit to make its transition from the earth plane to the afterlife. The symbols themselves were known to contain the activation of Sacred Energy. They were used as part of a complicated system of ritual to serve a purpose. The scribes themselves were considered high priests and, as such, were awarded the privilege of having their own tombs.

The word 'sacred' means holy, of a divine nature. This is not the same as 'secret', which means hidden. Sacred is unseen and only revealed when consciousness allows. Secrets cause negative human emotions. A sacred name has great spiritual potency. The Reiki symbols that Dr Usui transmitted at initiation contain great powers that unlock specific areas of consciousness to empower us with the ability to create stuff from non-stuff, whether that be healing the body, balancing relationships or giving empowerment to world situations.

There are three symbols for Second Degree. Along with each symbol is a mantra, which is the sound vibration of the symbol – its name. Within the name is contained the whole form of what it is and, by repeating the mantra with focused intent, the form comes into Being.

Wallace D Wattles describes the manifestations of stuff out of non-stuff beautifully in his book *The Science of Getting Rich* (with Dr J Powell). Firstly he describes the unmanifest – Universal Energy – …

> **There is a thinking stuff from which all things are made, and which, in its original state, permeates, penetrates, and fills the interspace of the Universe.**

… then our potential to influence it by the focus and intent of our mind …

> **A thought in Substance produces the thing that is imagined by that thought.**

... and further to the final manifestation ...

> *you can form things in your thoughts, and, by impressing your
> thoughts upon the Formless Substance, can cause the thing
> you think about to be created.*

That just about sums up Second Degree. The empowerment
of the unmanifest Universal Life Force, activated with intent and
specific mind stuff – symbol and mantra – created into manifest
Being. Magnificent! Now watch what you think!

So, once our thought is focused we can activate it into
being. This is where the three symbols come in. The first makes
a bridge between us and the person or situation we wish to
contact; the second contacts the mental and emotional
vibrational level; the third activates the process, empowers
it with motion in an ever-expanding direction. Energy moves
in a spinning spiral, from unlimited potential – via thought – into
being.

Life force + direction + activation = creation.
Energy + focus + intent = manifestation.

Uses of Second Degree Reiki

The most important area of focus is self-treatment. The second
is what underlies the global mind-set – human consciousness.
To treat our self is increasing consciousness of the whole.
In addressing human consciousness we are including our self.
For in essence we are it and it is us.

Second Degree Reiki can be used for:

1 Empowering the First Degree hands-on to go deeper more
   quickly. This may not be appropriate for everyone. The body
   must be present for this.
2 Instances when the body is not present (distant healing).
3 Individual physical, mental, emotional and spiritual healing,
   including children and animals.
4 Group healing.

5 Species of animals.
6 Areas of the world – conflict, war, famine, children, refugees, etc.
7 Situations – such as driving tests, exams, interviews, moving house, etc.
8 Relationships – between yourself and another, or a group, or other people's relationships.
9 People who are dying.
10 People who have died.
11 Spirits – this is not an area to enter into unless absolutely necessary as spirit entities are powerful invisible forces. They are so devious that they can disguise themselves as guides. Watch out, steer clear. Aim for the highest and bypass all mediators, including spirits, and tap into your own self-empowering inherent wisdom instead. By playing with spirits you give your power away and become weak.
12 Plants and species of plants.
13 The sending of love to our family.
14 The enhancement of prayer.
15 Self-treatment.

The process

First we sit somewhere quiet and comfortable, away from the children and the cat, away from the telephone and other pressing commitments. We take a minute to focus. Firstly the connection is made with the person requiring healing who has given permission. As the name is our personal mantra this is used to make contact. It does not have to be said out loud as the mind impression is a dynamic force and will link to the Being of the person wherever they are. Every invocation is repeated three times: this is to address the two levels of duality and contact the place of oneness. Father, Son and Holy Ghost, the two sides and the centre. The manifest, the unmanifest and the void.

Connection

We call their name three times. The person hears on an energetic level. By mental intention a thread of energy is sent out to the receiver, finding its way by matching the vibration and mantra. The thread is pulled back within the practitioner's own field without depleting the receiver or the giver.

The practitioner's field becomes a place of safety. The unity is available to the receiver like pranic food, or intravenous vitality!

The bridge is created

We call upon the first symbol to make a bridge between us and the person receiving. We call the mantra of the symbol three times and draw the symbol in the air once with the initiated hand. See the power of the priest as he draws the blessing of the cross above our heads.

Activation is then applied

We then call upon the activation symbol three times and draw it once to create the life force spin which moves energy in time and space. This process brings the essence of the receiver to us here in the present, so we can lay our hands on their invisible energy body. Out of this relationship manifests new messages. This symbol is not only the activator of energy but the creator of substance by its very nature. It works in a vortex, the densest part of which is matter itself.

Hands on – access to healing

There are many ways to keep the focus of this process but the easiest way is to place the person within yourself. We let the right leg represent the front of the person and divide it into three parts – the knee is the face and head, the mid-thigh is the centre of the body, the upper thigh is the hips, legs and feet. Likewise the left leg is divided to represent the back of the head, the back of the body and the back of the hips, legs and feet.

Figure 8.1 *Physical treatment at a distance.*

Place both hands on the right knee as corresponds to the head position; remain for a minute and a half – watch and wait. Notice what sensations and changes occur in the interface between the palm and the leg. From the moment we call the name, all sensations, symptoms and images are symbolic of the receiver in some way. Don't get too attached to these, however, as the important quality is that the Reiki is received. What we feel and see as possible psychic perceptions are just by-products. The hands are applied to the energy body which is directly linked to the unified field. The field of the practitioner expands to embrace that of the receiver.

We spend five minutes in this way on the front of the body and also the back of the body. When this is complete, we have accessed the energy field for that person via their own energetic and physical body.

The disposition

We call upon the mental/emotional symbol three times and draw it once in the air. This locks it onto the level of mind, emotion and subjective individuality. We then activate this energy level by again calling upon the activation symbol three times and drawing it out once.

Figure 8.2 *Mental/emotional treatment at a distance.*

We now hold the hands up, palms facing out (see above) with the fingers close and forming one unit, like radar dishes. They not only provide the access for Reiki to be drawn through, but also allow information to be received as to the quality of energy of the person, and sometimes even clues as to what else may be needed for their total well-being.

We invoke openness in the receiver by calling upon the affirmation three times – 'Divine Order, Harmony and Openness'. This gives access to the Divine Consciousness which is in perfect harmony and openness to receive it into their Being and personality, mind and emotions, to create change. We do not impose our ideas, thoughts or beliefs on them in any way.

We remain still for about five minutes watching and waiting. The quality of this energy can vary tremendously from person to person according to the depth of their illness or depression. It is often in this stillness that we recognize that energy is the only basic reality in our world. Our vision and perception begin to change the more we practise and let go.

Gratitude

At completion of the process we cross the hands over as before with gratitude and thanks. This process is so simple.

It takes 15 minutes to give a full body, mental and emotional level treatment to a person at a distance. By crossing over the hands and detaching from the treatment this sends the energetic body 'home' and separates us from the receiver, so that no residue is left within us and they remain complete also. This process is vital as it is protection from remaining merged. When the short session is over the practitioner breaks with the field and the thread, thereby sending it back home to the receiver with the change of Chi. The energy continues to draw in from the unified field even after the process is complete. The session acts as a catalyst for a new speed of function.

So to sum up:
* Obtain permission.
* Call the name three times.
* Call the bridge mantra three times. Draw the symbol once.
* Call the activation mantra three times. Draw once.
* Hands on.
* Call the disposition mantra three times. Draw once.
* Call the activation mantra three times. Draw once.
* Access energy through the hands up.
* Call Divine Order, Harmony and Openness three times.
  Let go.
* Close with crossed hands and thanks.

The full body treatment takes only five minutes for the front and five minutes for the back, during which time many signals, symbols and symptoms may be detected through our hands or in ourselves. It is possible to feel the full extent of the pain or emotion of the receiver in our own body, but this dissipates once we disconnect ourselves at the end with the process of giving gratitude. The essential body returns home to the physical body, taking with it any residue.

Reiki
Master's
degree

Reiki First and Second Degrees are usually enough for most people but some wish to take it further and learn more about themselves. Some even desire to teach others. The Master's level is a lifetime commitment which starts with the practice of a unique meditation technique, the Master's initiation, and continues with a three-year apprenticeship that gives the student the ability to transmit the knowledge of Reiki together with the empowerment of the initiations on others. Master's 1 is personal practice and Mastery. Master's 2 is the teacher-training element and involves organizing classes and learning what happens behind the scenes as well as being a professional practitioner. The lineage and traditions of this particular form must be honoured and unchanged if the student is to be accepted and given this incredible gift.

Master's Level 1 – Personal Mastery

This is a level purely for personal growth. It only enhances practice on others by the deep lateral view that evolves through regular practice. Reiki is a spiritual discipline which must be practised as such at this level. This means that dedication and commitment are necessary, not only to the regular practice of self-treatment, but also to the investigation of the ways of energy and the meaning of consciousness.

The Master level is triggered by initiation, during which the Master's symbol is implanted in the heart of the student. The seed of light grows and shines from within. Inner light burns away all unwanted emotions from the past and present, leaving a clear state. When the light shines from within we obtain enlightenment. As long as we see the light shining on us from without then we will live with a dark shadow. A technique of activation and empowerment is taught prior to the initiation to prepare the student, like tilling the soil and feeding it well before the chosen seed is planted. The heart must be truly ready for this and open to the deeply sacred nature of the process.

Master's Level 2 – Teacher Training

The pathway to becoming a Reiki-teaching Master should be one of a long apprenticeship having first prepared with the appropriate intervals between First, Second and Third Degree. I would not begin to consider anyone for training until they had been practising Reiki for at least three years. The apprentice teacher will organize and assist on a minimum of six First Degree classes and four Second Degree classes and will attend all reviews. A teacher must also have clinical experience as they will be teaching many therapists, nurses, doctors, etc., and needs to have witnessed first-hand the effects of long-term treatment. In-depth case histories may be required. Practice on others gives insight into the many possibilities of how different people heal from the same symptoms or diagnosed illness in such different ways. Each person is wholly unique and symptoms cannot describe their personality or way of living accurately. For teaching, many principles must be realized that cannot simply be described.

It is important that the Master endeavours to remain fit, well and in balance to be an example to the student. They must be able to maintain their own strength and grounding through trust and faith in the practice of this system. They must present themself in a professional way. They need confidence and conviction which only comes about through the experience of a guided apprenticeship.

Practice management is necessary, as is knowledge of treatment/training environment, equipment (you need several benches), ethics (non-discriminatory behaviour), group management, running of business, marketing, accounts, bookkeeping, publicity and giving talks. Organization skills are also necessary to arrange classes and this is a prerequisite for apprentice Masters. It is not quite as easy as people just turning up. Students, before learning, need nurturing as great change is afoot and many have fears and apprehensions.

Principles must be learnt, understood, practised and maintained in the Master's own life. Standards must be kept and honour given.

The best start would be to gain a Teacher Training Certificate from your local college. The Reiki Master's programme is mostly about Reiki, whereas the college courses offer an understanding through practical experience and observation to teach confidently any number of people in any situation.

Legal aspects must be understood, insurance obtained for public liability and malpractice. Presentational skills need to be learnt and practised for introductory talks, interviews, demonstrations, etc.

Aftercare of the student must be on hand. Sharing groups can be set up where students can review the technique and discuss any questions or experiences. Second Degree students are usually skilled enough to do this, seeing the group organization as an honour.

The Master's exchange must be made over a mutually agreed time, say three years. The exchange was set by Takata in the late

1970s at $10,000 or the equivalent currency exchange in your area. This is a lot. The commitment is even greater than this as it is a lifetime. This amount is payable in instalments as the apprentice Master runs their own classes. So the Reiki generates the exchange for you. After completion of this task the apprentice is free of commitment to their trainer but never free of the commitment to uphold the principles of preparation, exchange, number of symbols, number of initiations, simplicity and the meaning of sacred.

Method to invoke energy

In Japan this technique is known as Hatsurei HO. 'Hatsu' is to invoke or generate, 'rei' is spirit or energy and 'ho' is method or way – the 'method to invoke energy'. This was traditionally only given to teaching Reiki Masters but it is now taught at other stages. This method to invoke energy is performed by the teaching Reiki Master prior to initiating, and prior to their personal daily self-treatment. It is not taught at Reiki Level 1 or Reiki Level 2 as keeping things simple is best in the early stages. It will, however, be taught at Masters Level 1, Masters Level 2, and during the Empowerment through Advanced Reiki Practice programme for self-treatment.

1 Posture – begin by standing in a relaxed posture or seated upright with the eyes closed.
2 Preparation – allow the mind a frew moments to quieten.
3 Hand posture – 'Gassho' in Japanese, 'mudra' in Indian – hands together as if in prayer position. This aligns the energy forces in the hands, creating calmness and a focus back within the body.
4 Bow – as a sign of respect – open the hands out as if to receive something then repeat in the mind three times 'I open the door and enter'.
5 Intention – focus mental awareness on the present.
6 Energy seep – place the right-hand palm at the left shoulder about an inch above the surface. Sweep down the body diagonally to the right hip and beyond in a gentle but

sharp flicking motion (as in a martial art 'block'). Repeat three times.

7 Repeat with the left hand just above the surface from the right shoulder to the left hip and beyond. Repeat three times.

8 Place the right hand at the left shoulder with the left arm straight out in front, sweep down just above the surface of the arm energetically and flick off beyond the hand (on a bare arm this will feel like a wind blowing on the arm). Repeat three times.

9 Place the left hand at the right shoulder sweeping down as above. Repeat three times.

10 Both arms are raised straight above the head pointing to the sky without strain. Notice any sensations in the hands.

11 Place the hands in the lap, palms facing upwards. Notice any sensations in the hands.

12 Conscious breath – notice, without strain, as the breath comes in and goes out. Notice the point at which the breath turns from out to in and from in to out and is neither in nor out but suspended for a moment. The quieter the mind, the slower the breath and the longer the gaps will be.

13 As the breath comes inwards, imagine breathing light from outside yourself, down through the top of the head into the whole body. Breathe out naturally and breathe in the light again for a further two breaths.

14 Breathe in as 13 but imagine the light radiating out through the hands on the out breath. Repeat for three breaths.

15 At this point Reiki precepts can be repeated three times each on the out breath to remind yourself of your qualities.

16 Alternatively, just sit quietly and become aware of the energy within and in the hands.

17 Practise the self-treatment programme or the attunements at this point.

18 Hand posture – 'Gassho' as above. Repeat three times in the mind, 'I give thanks and close the door'.

19 Bow in completion and open the eyes.

The downward flick in this method creates a flow of Chi down from the top of the arm and out through the hands in order to activate the Reiki for the treatment or attunements. In the finishing off technique (Chapter 6), the flick is generated upwards towards the heart in order to gather the energy back within the body and centre the person after the treatment.

Master's requirements – checklist

* Reiki 1 Certificate with bona fide Master.
* Reiki 2 Certificate with bona fide Master not less that three months from Reiki 1.
* Fulfil practitioner requirements as set out in Chapter 10.
* Complete apprenticeship training including Master's Level 1.
* Complete or commit to full Master energy exchange.
* Hold a teaching certificate.
* Have full malpractice and public liability insurance.
* Commit to continued professional development.
* Honour the commitment to confidentiality and ethics.
* Above all maintain a professional standard.

Questions to ask your potential master

* What is Reiki? Can they be clear and concise?
* What is your historical lineage? They should be able to trace back in line to Dr Usui and not be more than five, six or seven in line from Takata.
* Do you teach the history of Reiki?
* How long was your training?
* How long was your apprenticeship?
* How much did you pay? If their energy exchange was only a few hundred pounds or dollars and their training a day or a weekend only, then they do not understand the quality of this energy.
* What is the name of your Master's Master?
* How soon after First Degree will I be able to take Second Degree and how much do these levels cost?

* Will I be able to take the Master's Level?
* Can I go into practice straight away?
* How many symbols do you teach for Second Degree and Master's Level 1? If more than three for Second or one for Master's then question the origin of the others and claims of channelling from Usui and Takata.
* How many initiations do you perform for each level? There should be four for First and one each for Second Degree and the Masters.
* Do you include the legs and feet in the finishing-off technique for grounding? This is asked as many teachers omit the legs and feet, thus leaving the receiver ungrounded and spaced out.
* How many Masters have you trained? One to three should have taken them through nine years of their practice. Be suspicious if this Master boasts 20 or several hundred.
* Have you been in public practice?
* Do you practise on yourself?
* Do you teach the five precepts?
* How much do you charge? Charges will vary from country to country but should at least be in line with any other professional training.
* Do you take other forms of exchange?
* Do you belong to any Reiki organization?
* Are you insured to practise and teach? With whom?
* How many people are taught in a class? There should be no more than 12 for an individual teacher or 20 with a Second Degree assistant. Personal contact is imperative and cannot be given in groups of 50.

Ask for a trial treatment from the Master or one of their professional students. Experiencing Reiki first-hand is the best way to decide. Be prepared to travel: come to me, I will teach you.

10

Reiki in practice

Being a Reiki Therapy practitioner is a responsibility not to be taken lightly. There is as lot to learn alongside the actual technique. There are codes of conduct, ethical policies, business, tax, health and safety issues, and learning to integrate Reiki with other therapies. Personally I feel Reiki is a stand-alone therapy and should be given by itself, in order to benefit fully from the elements of stillness and silence that are an essential part of the healing process.

Other techniques can be learnt that complement Reiki and each person needs to find the combination that best suits their needs. Reiki can amplify the effects of other techniques and is always useful for the therapist self-treating at the end of a busy day. Reiki complements treatment with orthodox medicine and gives people the ability to help reduce their levels of stress and therefore perhaps lesser the need for intervention.

As much as self-treatment and treating others is important, receiving treatment from a professional Reiki therapist is extremely rewarding. Through professional training, the therapist will have gained other skills to help guide you through the process of healing and be able to explain the sensations and feelings that can arise. It is also of great comfort to share this experience within a safe environment where you can return, to go further, or deeper as you wish. Self-treatment is then invaluable to assist the process between treatments. The practitioner may be able to guide you to find more courage and hope as the physical symptoms begin to lessen.

Procedure

Before you think about setting up as a Reiki therapist, you should consider the following:
* Perform daily self-treatment.
* Keep a journal of experiences and changes.
* Perform regular full treatments on others.
* Take people through a course of treatments, perhaps ten people through three to ten treatments each.
* Learn to take case histories and keep notes of treatments on others.
* Commit to Second Degree with daily practice of distant healing.
* Undertake a programme of supervised treatments.
* Record case studies in a portfolio.
* Attend support groups and revision sessions as part of continued professional development.
* Complete and maintain a First Aid Certificate.
* Learn basic anatomy and physiology.
* Learn basic communication and counselling skills and study the client–therapist relationship.
* Set boundaries of time, commitment, exchange, professional relationship.
* Look into practice management – taking a course, investing in equipment, i.e. bench, covers, clinical rent,

clothing, blanket, diary, etc., accounts, bookkeeping, record of money.
* Personal hygiene – no cigarettes or garlic, no strong perfume or incense.
* Business cards, leaflets, appointment cards.
* Become apprentice to a practitioner mentor.
* Insurance – check the laws in your country.
* Ethics – this is a very involved subject and must be looked into in detail.

As a therapist it is not our place to divulge our insight into the client's illness, but knowing what we may know we can guide them towards the realization for themselves. Once they hit upon the understanding through their own experience the energy can shift and transformation instantly occurs. The therapist must guide towards the gift, not give the answers.

Treatment in practice is more involved than just the simple laying on of hands with the intention to heal. So firstly practise on yourself, friends and family and gain confidence through the deep insight that will grow in you. Also it is wise to receive regular treatment from someone else. I do this myself by swapping with a friend and really notice the difference on the weeks she and I are too busy to get together.

Reiki as a complement to other therapies

Reiki is a complete system in itself. Additional techniques are not usually necessary as all utilize the same Universal Life Force. All complementary therapies aim to rebalance the energy by using different methods and principles but see the person as a whole. They look into the habits of the person, their likes and dislikes, their emotional history as well as the physical symptoms. All things together create the map of the individual in the state of current imbalance. Many people who learn Reiki go on to learn other forms of therapy and many people come to learn who already practise

(I also have a diploma in Indian Head Massage and am a certified practitioner of Emotional Therapy). The main importance is to note that their common experience is that Reiki becomes a protection for them during their other treatments, which, with massage, chiropractic, etc., can be quite tiring. Each practitioner has the gift to regenerate their own energy before, during or after treatment on another.

Many therapists use the Reiki in combination with their other forms of therapy and thus personal therapies evolve. Each person is drawn to a different combination of systems that they are led to by their own personal journey. As Reiki never leaves, it is available in the hands at all times and may come through during aromatherapy, reflexology or Zero Balancing treatments. Some practitioners like to keep each therapy separate and evolve from one skill to another as the client is ready for it. Sometimes it is found that some structural manipulation or alignment is useful before Reiki in order to allow deep healing to occur. I personally find that structural blocks can slow down the process quite dramatically. Generally, with trust and patience, the Reiki will shift all the levels. Reiki assists the integration of other systems and the smooth transition from illness to health.

Reiki is recommended to clients by counsellors of many forms: psychosynthesis, transactional analysis, Emotional Therapy, psychodrama, brief therapy, neuro-linguistic programming (NLP), hypnotherapy, and so on. By practising self-treatment daily the emotions and issues that arise during therapy can be integrated without such pain. Reiki transforms energy from one form to another without the need for the individual issue or memory being accessed. Many deep-seated blocks can leave the system without the need for them to be unearthed in the present only to cause the opening of a huge can of worms. The past can be such a pit of pain for some people but the transition can be eased with Reiki as it leads the Being and the body towards the light.

Reiki can enhance our ability for channelling, clairvoyance, mediumship, telepathy, and intuitive interpretation of Runes, Tarot and palmistry. Our basic insight awakens to see and know all things.

Reiki is used hand in hand with orthodox medicine by those brave enough to challenge the limitations of science. It has been found useful with therapies such as radiotherapy, chemotherapy, physiotherapy, hydrotherapy, vitamin therapy, nutritional therapy and general medical drug therapy. It helps patients reduce their stress levels, detoxify their systems and heal their injuries or illnesses more rapidly. The side-effects of chemotherapy and radiotherapy can be eased, including nausea, anxiety, exhaustion and the tension in scar tissue.

Recovery from surgery can be quite surprising, especially when the treatments begin some weeks before medical treatment commences. This prepares the person, the body and especially the site for the trauma. Treatment after surgery speeds up the tissue regeneration, easing shock and bruising. Distant Second Degree Reiki can be very effective in these circumstances. It gives the person waiting at home a valid role to play in an otherwise helpless situation.

Reiki experience varies from person to person, but it never ceases to amaze me how such a simple thing can produce such a profound effect that not only heals the physical wounds but changes people's lives into ones of joy and fulfilment. Treat yourself, take it further.

Further information

For courses in the British Isles and Europe with Reiki Master Sandi Leir-Shuffrey MFA, RMA, MUKRF, FAETC, FETcert, DipIHM, please contact her directly at the address below leaving your name, address and telephone number for information, or visit the website and send her an email.

Sandi Leir-Shuffrey
The Stillpoint School of Reiki
Mulberry Cottage
St Chloe Green
Amberley
Stroud
Gloucestershire GL5 5AP
England
Tel: (44) 01453 872575
Email: info@teachyourselfreiki.co.uk
www.teachyourselfreiki.co.uk